THE ONE RIGHT TOUCH
by
Katharine Coles

Ahsahta Press
Boise State University
Boise, Idaho

Acknowledgments

The following poems have appeared in the periodicals designated: "Donna Julia's First Letter," ***American Literary Review***; "Love Poem for the Nuclear Age," ***College English***; "Touring the Yucatan," ***Ellipsis***; "A Room With a View," ***The Georgia Review***; "Not a Storytelling Family," "My Mother's Lesson," ***The Memphis State Review***; "Letter From a Friend on Her Anniversary," ***The New Republic***; "Declension," ***Poetry Northwest***; "Kudzu," ***Prairie Schooner***; "Before Parting," "Father," ***Quarterly West***; "Demeter," ***Shenandoah***; "Sex as a Trope," ***Weber Studies***.

Thanks to the Utah Arts Council and the National Endowment for the Arts for their support for poems in this manuscript.

Editor for Ahsahta Press: Dale K. Boyer

The One Right Touch is printed on acid-free text and cover papers.

Second printing, May 1994

ISBN 0-916272-54-0

Library of Congress Catalog Card Number:
92-81877

Contents

Introduction

Laodicean with regard to almost *every* little thing which contributes to the stock wherewithal of our journalizing poetry, Ms. Coles's response is rather to elemental violence, even when it proceeds from mere mortals, relatives and lovers (those indispensable irrelevances), even when such violence is masked or belied. Yet we recognize these stark, staring poems most confidently when she acknowledges the depredations of sunlight, or the erasures of wind and water, the stars "keeping their violence at such a distance", and the mountains that

> hunker down in the night in a tension
> like courtship—the impulse to rise
> and the desire to fall
> all the same motion.

This poet is likely enough in her apprehensions of the art—notice how suavely the closed form writhes in her hands in "The Suicides," and how cunningly she assumes the voices, the drastic presences of imagined or remembered others. Yet these are the least *worldly* of any new poems I know, the least entangled in the household bonds of life. How Rilke would have praised her for that, who so deplored his own mundane imbroglios—how readily he would have attached the final poem here, an icy, cauterizing "Love Poem for the Nuclear Age," to the Duino project! For Katharine Coles is desperately concerned to set her adorations—and we must read this word in all its original senses: to speak, to plead, to pray, and most originally, *to pronounce a ritual formula*—on the page with just enough salt or ice or vinegar to keep them crisp or distinct (her effort is to be *in keeping*, to be decorous, seldom to be decorative). They are not imperishable, such ecstasies, the poet knows as much from her own experiments with keeping, and so she goes about forming structures and figures which—for the most part irregular, sorrowing, variable—will stand as *spectacular ruins* (e.g. her signature poem, "Touring the Yucatan"). Adoration, in terms of the pervasive vehemence of the landscape Out West, is quite as easily phrased in terms of execration, the turnabout *immaterial*.

In such eager extremities, Ms. Coles repeatedly calls to mind certain religious women who have made their statements (their orations, then) as the *trace* of their enterprise rather than as its purpose or goal; women who like that Spanish saint required a certain fragmentation of the spirit before they could submit to its gale force; women who, in their wilderness of elemental havoc, would implore with Ms. Coles:

>   let every thing
> given to guard me
> fall through my fingers.

In such writing, the signs are always reversible, and only what is perceived as broken can be prophesied as whole; only what is castigated can be endured as joy; only what is jeopardized is free.

Richard Howard
New York City
January, 1992

*For my parents, Joan and William Coles,
and for Chris Johnson, my husband*

I.

A Room with a View

When the lake freezes across
they drive out for miles, he said,
Jeeps and old pick-ups
loaded with saws, coolers, boxes
of intricate tackle. They drop their lines
right out the car windows.
The skaters, their bright sons,
flash all afternoon over the inlets,

and at last, made brave by motion
and their own heat, dash for the center—
only ice, snow coming on, dusk
dulling the surface. He didn't tell it
quite this way, and there is no lake here,

where I look out, elbows on the sill.
But I imagine the music
each radio gives, and the fish, slow,
lifting toward the ice, their blood
as cold as the water that buoys them.

Behind me, he bathes
and serenades in his deepest voice.
I hold myself still—already his smallest word
can wrench me open, as if it's our love
that has finished or failed
and the scene taken me. Pink neon,

the Downtowner Bar flares across the glass,
but beyond, I know, mountains
hunker down in the night, in a tension

like courtship—the impulse to rise
and the desire to fall
all the same motion. The men
lean on their pick-up horns in symphony.
The boys tumble from the shadows and light snow

and lift the creel lids,
their dinners eyeing them coldly.
I want that lake as he saw it
but I settle for my own view:
headlights flash on
and move toward the white shores
and forests, toward the kitchens
where women tie on aprons and test knives
against their thumbs. One watches
her face turn in the window
and imagines in it a world

before grief—her then careless body
approaching violence, hands
making her surface dance. Her fingers
turn the knife—all the colors of silver,
the scales lift; the pale flesh
tears open. Her husband

pats her as he passes, his touch
almost absent—like the touch of the man
who will walk out of the bath, turn on the light.
Come away from the window, he'll say,
his hands on my waist. It's dark.
There's nothing to see.

Declension

I didn't touch him as we walked the garden's paths,
fall, maples and the shrubbery in ruins,
but you and my body have your own imaginations,

so later I pulled the blinds against the thinning light,
old men stuttering through the trash piled at curbside,
hookers who shouted across the cement park

or leaned into sedan windows, knelt at open car doors.
Infidelity, casual consent: that day, I believed
that a man may look to a woman for everything—flesh,

beyond flesh. He and I both had talk about love
behind us: you, the one whose faith I broke for you,
others who had broken us pushed aside for the moment.

*

Did you think I would never stray beyond your courtyard?
Sun, brick, almost buoyant impatiens and pale drinks,

every face placid and tan under shifting leaves,
a man bent to a pitcher of liquid, spinning ice. You recall

only the moment you turned holding a full glass for me,
and later the floral sheets folded down, cool,

our bodies coming together languorous,
almost abstracted. I could show you a home I've made apart

but you believe in the life you keep for me
in your quiet house, sure of what you wait for.

*

Oh, this wanderlust, cities' lights from the air
unwinding like pinwheels. This new desire
is more than I want, but I travel for it anyway.

On his nightstand, late pears, numbers luminous as signs.
Never has this hour, light closing down into evening,
seemed so permanent, my body humming

as if with his life, as if I could fold into his hands
and let them coax any shape from me—a weightless arch,
a long-necked bird with her head thrown back.

*

I thought there was little wrong with my life:
you kept at a distance, in a courtyard memory encloses

in light. Except for what you and my body imagine, I have
what I wanted. Solitude. Avocados growing dull on the sill.

But my heart makes this privacy suddenly imperfect,
as if the birds that whistle and chuckle from the hedge

had stopped to wait for some sign from me, and the house
fell silent. I am tired of telephones, voices traveling

too easily, as if any of us cared about speech now.
Distracted, we pick up anything to fill our hands—

tall glasses, sweating, the pears or icy apples.
No more of this. I must stop believing

I can articulate my heart to you,
this dumb muscle, bad company.

*

On the subway platform, he teaches me to juggle:
apple, red army knife, apple again
poised above the graffiti—you've seen this trick.

I am miles from any home. Not even you
can discover me in the subterranean light,
so on the train I sway into him

and press the blade to the fruit,
one bright surface giving to the other,
the skin a clean spiral falling away.

Provisions

Hunting

The window over the bed
left open. Half in sleep,
I think I'm in the tent

waking early. Father up already,
his tin cup steaming.
The campfire a long

bright moment in a morning
all one color: pale sky, ground
mist rising, husks of flowers

and grass limned with frost. The city
just a dream—lights rising,
dark orchards all around.

Cultivation

A song or a joke. Dead skunk
in the middle of. Why did
the skunk cross? Out

in the orchard, plodding
from windfall to windfall,
he felt this snow

coming on. Tucked into one
last apple. Looked
to the highway, all

its flash and whir
and his dark den beyond.
On the shoulder, I teeter

on dangerous party shoes.
The man driving me
kneels in his best trousers

and works his knife up
under the skin. Draws it
slow through the soft belly.

Gathering

November, and still
there are roses. Not even
black yet with frost. My neighbor's,

not mine. I want
to touch whatever
catches my eye. Let everything

given to guard me
fall through my fingers. All summer
I've watched them. How

they don't resist. I keep
thinking it's over but more
push out and open and fall.

Cultivation, 2

In the light from the high-beams
he scrapes back the fur. Locates
and trims off the scent glands.

Pulls the pelt up, the inch
of winter fat reluctantly peeling.
He's never believed

in waste. He shakes out the hide.
Folds it into the bag.
Scrubs his hands

lightly in the snow. Walks back, touches
my hair, tightens my scarf
gently to my throat.

Gathering, 2

Thief. According to story
the oldest profession: in the garden
she must have begun

by gathering flowers.
Then berries from brambles
right at hand level. Then

of one mind she reached
for the ripe fruit
just overhead, the apple's descent

into gravity. Her mind
was never so simple
again. I lean

to my neighbor's roses,
their fragrance still
more than I bargained for.

Cultivation, 3

So we are late
and cold. Orion
wheels in his

continuous hunt. Bright
anyway in the sky.
Inside, candleflame

blurs into haloes
on the steamed windows.
He goes to wash his hands

again. I move in
among the women under chandeliers.
Mirrors flash us

back, red and emerald
silks caught only
for a moment in the glass,

necklaces shining.
Light's delicate lines
on our skin. The host

squeezes my hands, scrapes
his cheek over mine. The men
shift in their dark suits

or pause, caught
by a word, a head
lifting. Their hands move

over our waists, shoulders—
a sash, a lock of hair
too neat or gone astray.

Hunting, 2

The city just a dream—
I move through
the woods, my red hat,

red parka blazing
among the pines. Gunfire popping.
Limbs laden

with the last red and yellow
leaves flare in my arms,
in the white air

as they will against
my flat, white walls.
Miles away, my father,

pocket lunch long gone,
lifts his rifle. The doe
lowers her head

to the tree's tender bark.
Her body the only dream
she's ever had—that

and the body moving through hers
heavy in spring as she works
back to high country.

Cultivation, 4

I edge toward the punchbowl.
The hostess follows
with dips on a tray, little

corncobs and mushrooms. She shows me
the curios, her father's
carved figures. Kenyan ivory

going to yellow—
the shapes of elephants,
trunks raised, tusks

carved in ebony, black against
pale, stylized flesh. Her finger
tracks the cuts and grooves.

In his absence, she says,
she would arrange the figures
on her nightstand. Drop

to sleep among them,
small and dangerous
and afraid in the tall grasses.

Hunting, 3

Miles from camp
he guts her. Leaves
the entrails for someone

else to read. He is hungry.
He imagines the doe
hanging by her feet in the carport,

himself and his friends gliding
hunting knives over her, loving
the feel of that

serious business. Hide
pulled away, she will be
only smooth, her graceful

swells and tucks mauve
behind translucent membrane,
the delicate lacing of fat.

Gathering, 3

Ripe fruit in the bowl. The end
of the meat on the platter. After supper
I walk the neighborhood.

The roses now really
finishing. Twilight
when I reach the orchards—

all year I've taken
branches in bloom, ripe
and fallen fruit. Soon

snow will cover everything—
the ground, the branches—
in half-dark like blossoms

making their own light. So I close
my hands on themselves, pocket
the full harvest against the cold.

Arson

for L.M., 1959-1975

You were right. There's nothing sacred
in our bodies, these houses decaying,
neighborhoods let go to sag and ruin.
The trashbin must have smoldered
all day on the back stair—
afternoon of rain, smell of mold,
wet earth—before the flame
licked out the rear wall of the row houses,
all now lit within, identical,
walls blackening, sparks aloft over the bare
yards. We drove slow past mothers
and children in pajamas, huddled together,
leaning on trees, cars, each other's shoulders,
watching their porches list and one by one
give in. You said you wanted to

leave your flesh, the way the fire leaps
rooftop to rooftop—did you really think
there'd be another body waiting for you to burn?
Later in the garage, the car barely moving you,
the exhaust rising to your head,
you must have hoped your soul would lift,
weightless and whole,
from your body. We are years away, years past

the drive down the flaming avenue.
You smiled and kissed each of us,
walked inside, turned off the porch light.
The next morning in the halls at school
we held against the day's lesson.
Our bodies could collapse on their own
empty chambers, brilliant then dark.
I still wake from a street

blazing on both sides, a tunnel of fire
as far as the *eye can see*. I shift in bed
or rise to the window for a sign
night's lifting. Dark still hides the hand
holding the match. It could strike anywhere,
sputtering in cupped palms and flaring, the days
burning down, the house consumed from within
and myself at the curb in my thin gown,
my face flickering in the flickering light.

My Mother's Lesson

In the car, she shifts down
  and leans to the wheel,
in her throat rising scales
  the teacher will pull
through her all
  morning. She enters

her body's tentative music,
  her voice faltering
upward: she wants to discover
  how some, in tune,
work inward and bring out
  the notes joined

as if they had always meant
  to gather into sound
out of nothing. At a stoplight
  she looks around—
a schoolyard gritty with snow,
bare trees and wires,

and on the corner a man
  she has not seen before,
and a pistol shoulder-high,
  apparently trained
on her blue silk scarf. Calm,
  she shifts, pulls through

the unchanged red light
  and is gone,
the man behind her now
  and his gun
unchanged, still
  silent, the only explosion

the one she sounds and re-
  sounds in her mind,
and only, that—none
  of love's tensions
or wounds between them, no
  jealousy, dissonant

notes. An enigma. Blocks
  away, she glances
back, drives on—nothing, she says,
  left to chance.
At her lesson, she starts,
  stumbles, and the metronome

counts her beyond her own
  compromising rhythm
and this is the best she's ever
  sung: abandoned
to the rise, the dying fall,
  her voice loosens

a music she has always felt
  playing through
her body's cadence. She carries
  one phrase so wide
it presses her ribcage, opens
  her throat, climbs

into the sweet, dangerous
  air of release,
her voice pushing past
  notes recklessly,
reclaiming moment after
  free moment, exactly

as they occur to her.

Father

I imagined all the bright lights I could
for him—an old movie-set hotel,
neon glaring on the wall at dusk,
hat and tails laid out on the bed,
his white gloves flashing. I embroidered
handkerchiefs, dreamed him pressing them
to the eyes of women unlike my mother,
their bodies in the darkness white
and flickering, or vivid in casinos
where they turned their heads bright as birds
whose plumage warns of bitter
or dangerous flesh. His failure
was in what he gave me—the trimmed
suburban shrubbery, the swingset
erected in the snow one Christmas—
so I gave him low, black cars,
told my friends how their curves glowed
under streetlights. I lost myself
in leather and furs, the upholstery
where women laid back their heads
laughing, their throats quivering
and so white, so tender in the darkness
I thought his touch would bruise them.
My friends turned their faces
on my pillow and touched my hair,
their eyes moist with love
for the father I'd made, created
whole from the midwestern boy who'd stepped
blinking from his mother's schoolhouse
into the fifties' regulated light. For him
I wanted the drama of a heartbreak
he had earned, one that had left him
stranded in the life I knew
he had built with such care, for me,
sadness by accumulated, ordinary sadness.

Letter from a Friend on Her Anniversary

As always in fall I dream the house burns
and I walk toward him all night through flaming rooms

leaving you behind as if you were myself
calling me back. Sometimes I sit with him

all night on the lawn, watching the planets
and remote stars keeping their violence

at such a distance. We wait
until daylight. Across the street, girls arrive

in pairs for early service, their pale eyes still
and wide, looking past us, past the church,

away from this world, bright with longing.
They don't need to see how autumn burns

their city, across the foothills, the horizon,
the cold sky. This world is nothing to them.

They will never die. We pull down the last of the bottle
and think perhaps we could sleep soon.

He touches my cheek, the bruises
still rising as they did that night

when I told you it doesn't matter.
Believe me, I don't shy

from his hand. I wait for it
to coax a blush, a bruise, blood

where the skin gives. It's all the same
in love. In the house, the drapes lift

as in a breeze, our figures shadows
of the flame. If I turned and ran

what could I save? Only my body, dry tinder
that catches for him. My good friend,

for him, for the one right touch,
I will lie to you. You know I have always been bad

at my life, and that it is all I have.

Sex as a Trope

Down, hands flat
to the earth, the loam
she feeds and coaxes

life from, she knows
as if by sight what roots
thicken below—carrots

growing brilliant, potatoes,
rich turnips. She wipes
her hands on her shirttails,

goes in, takes a stiff brush
to her nails, aching,
packed with dirt. The rain

arrives as predicted.
Light wavers like water
through the potted herbs

gone wild on her windowsill.
She pinches mint for tea,
lays out her cup, the kettle

on the burner. She will rock
awhile by the window. Rain
pushes at the glass like wasps

on those chilly days in autumn.
The way, she thinks, a woman
pushes herself against

the surface of the world,
as if it might open
into shelter, a small, light place.

*

He tells her how the girl
bent down her head,
her sleeve and collar torn,

how she touched her eyelid,
pushed almost shut
and still darkening, touched

her swollen lips, her whole face
grown beyond itself
to one she couldn't find

her own in. He thinks
she felt sorry for that stranger,
reached her hand

to the mirror, a gesture
all the comfort she had
to offer. He says it was only

what it was. A girl
wept before the mirror.
She unbuttoned her blouse

again for the camera. Hard,
the lights revealed no more
than they were meant to. A document,

ways a touch can blossom.
He says the men spoke
gently to her. Asked her

to turn. Turn again.
They are used to the turns
love takes. The woman wonders

how long the bruises
would show. How much longer
every touch would hurt.

*

Gravity. Bodies come together
and spin free, wheeling off

into time's inexplicable curve.
Explicable, then. The universe

as a loaf of bread rising.
But what's bread

that can't be tasted, smelled
coming out of the oven? Bonehead

Astronomy, she remembers. Physics
for the simple, who understand

what they touch. Is it the future
or the past that draws her

from bed to window?
What's the difference, if it all

curves back on itself?
Star bright, but the sky

is full of stars tonight
and she can't say which

first caught her eye. Star light,
it carries old news quickly,

the message changing with distance,
the speed of retreat.

Even the sun and earth,
so intimate, miss each other

again and again. Even
the heavenly bodies fly

apart as fast as they can.
Now, in her body

rising separate into the night,
or when she escapes her body in sleep,

she likes this hurtling
through space, this going away

fast. Star bright. She sends
her wish to all of them.

*

Remember a little
torn-up garden. Shrubs

laid bare, their clipped tops
strewn on the walks. Everything

cut and tied for autumn.
The grass widened out

to a park, still green,
and the birds hopped

from sunlight to sunlight
as if the late warmth meant

summer might stay. The food was simple—
thick bread, cheese, pears

and the last grapes passed palm
to fingertip, mouth to mouth.

Because of its gravity
they took the world

lightly, as the leaves had
all summer, turning

above the lawns and swept stones.
And suddenly the wind

pulled them free—leaves
spinning fast to the ground

or lifting on intricate drafts.
Red, bright yellow, the air

whirled with leaves, and they both
turned spread-eagle

on their backs, mouths open,
glad for the fall.

He tells her he took
his daughter to the carnival.
Vendors. The young

in their Saturday motley, bright
and threadbare. The rides whirled,
silly with lights and music.

For once he watched the men.
The women, as always, passed by
as if in the distance, self-

possessed. Their feet turned out
gently, he says, in that way
women's feet have, and their throats

were damp in the heat. He wanted
to reach out and touch
their napes, just touch them

where their hair clung
in tendrils escaping
those bright clasps—but as he said

he was watching the men:
they craned after the women;
some would turn for a moment

and walk backwards, watching.
He tells her
they made noises. Growls

low in their throats. Hoots.
Or just their mouths
working, growing moist. The women—

he'd never noticed before—
looked at no one.
Or rather, they turned

only their eyes now and again,
as if asking directions, as if
to catch glimpses of themselves.

*

She falls awake,
clinging to the sheets,

then climbs the long ladder back.
She dreams to get things right,

and over with. Cold
that spreads. Poison,

dinner gone badly. Surrender
to fire, fever, passion,

all the same. To the touch
of a stranger, the caress of one

who loves her too much
to let her escape,

tonight, into dreams, or tomorrow
into her own life. She wonders

if it matters whose hands,
another's or her own, carry her

roughly into the night.
The end will come

violent after all—if not in pain
or wrenching light, or even

in flames swelling her, then
in her body surrendered to time

as it's always been. It is
everything to her, and nothing.

II.

Donna Julia's First Letter
After Juan's Departure for Cadiz

Isabella, more and more I remember childhood
and you lifting your petticoats under the arbor

just to feel the sun on you. It is late summer.
We have finished our studies. The governess sleeps
on the shaded bench surrounded by roses. Remember

what happened next? By now, I know you have heard
my story—even you, in the cloisters
where I am going. My choice will end me

there, near God and you, whom I've lied to.
My virtue was so easy all those years

it was safe: a husband too old for much,
my own body trained to forget itself.
And I had grown as good a shrew as any.

I will travel as far within the convent walls
as he, as far as I ever did between my husband's house

and Donna Inez's garden with its trellises,
its fleshy hanging flowers. How she dangled
before me that boy plumping into ripeness,

his rich skin and delicate fingers
like yours—even his *eyes*, coquette's eyes like yours,

those fabulous lashes shading the danger.
A fan, a veil—what a flirt I could have made him!

It is bad manners for a woman to love
too much, to lose to passion what helps her
button her body in, button her whole self

with steady fingers, bind up silk and lace,
button after button, her head lowered,
her lashes lowered over her eyes, working

in perfect containment. Now I will walk in
from the stifling sun to that labyrinth of cells,
the stone walls everywhere cool and damp.

I will reach out to the stones' caress.
I will press my body against them, there

in the cool, almost darkness of midday.
I will cultivate the habit, draw its folds
down over my shoulders; bare

and mobile all day under rough cloth
my nipples will grow tender then raw

with passion; I will know
the feel of this flesh, the life I take
in my own hands all night. Bella,

and I will end well! When I finish this
I am ready. I will write him

on gilt-edged paper, with the seal
I use for you—*elle vous suit partout*—
the right lies about a woman's one love

and passion, a lady's diminutive tragedy.
My last decorous act, which he may let go
to whatever wind he pleases. Bella, no tears.

Not a Storytelling Family

In that old house she'd made over
my mother would lean at the window,

the kettle forgotten in her hand,
and look east past the bluing mountains

and all the wide-open plains
to a street she'd once strolled down singing,

swinging her arms, wishing she could stay.
I never asked what she'd lost—

the childhood spent moving landscape
to landscape: Jakarta's jungle,

airy Costa Rica, Cuba in its vivid seas.
Even my father pulled her loose

from an old city, almost
familiar ghosts, declining gardens,

cousins whose hands she'd finally touched.
By then she must have learned

to walk away, not to hold
anything and rub it, a charm repeated,

polished from use like the tales
my friends' parents and grandparents told—

the whole cast, nodding, revised
the evenings and bright, wrenching days,

the years the world kept growing
but the smells of woodsmoke and supper

still called them home. Speaking,
the tellers grew distant, perfect

as their pasts, myths true
in every version. My mother turned

her face to the present,
and I invented her life,

how she and my father drove out
of their old, industrial city and west

to drift in all that space—prairies
repeating for days, scorched brush,

the sun glinting pale and dangerous
off the Chevy's dusty fins. I saw them

wind down through the mountains at last
and step into our street,

the row of white houses. Begonias flared
on the shaded porches for years.

Like my friends' great-grandmothers,
my mother sat down on her steps and swore

she would never pack up again. I knew
this story as if she had told it—how

the water tasted in midwestern towns
and countries my friends had never heard of,

everything but what she must have
most remembered, all

left behind. I never said what I
left to search for: the cities

that had passed through her, her face
exotic on the dirty waterfronts,

village squares pale and hot at midday,
cobbled streets turned

to dust at the edge of town.
I travel all the way back

and touch my mother's arm. She starts,
fills the kettle and lights the stove.

We pass the afternoon talking
of food, the long days, what we carry

into this moment, and the next. Anything
but what she leaves as she turns away

to set out the cups—the past and its growing,
unmapped wilderness.

Sentimental

for my brothers

The rains will move in today.

We carry umbrellas into the sunlight,
down paths we walked together
as earnest children, longing to be grown
and far away. At three we stroll
again to chapel. Watch dust
float through the bright
bodies of saints glazing the windows.

Growing, we believed
what we were told. Nothing
could stay. Not love. Not any particular
angle of sun, our own senses sure
to fade, maybe before the world's
certain turn from sense.

We move again
in a wild light. This desert
is so brilliant we return as if
to our lives. But the scorpion's
delicate manners make her stunned prey
last for days. The creosote's
poisonous roots insure it
life and solitude. These names
we remember from paradise: Bright Angel Trail, Garden
of Eden. After each brief rain, ephemerals
burst into exuberant life. Dark Angel,
Devil's Garden, Fiery Furnace. Alone
on foot, we have lost ourselves
in mazes of canyons. We might have died of thirst.
We stay near camp and lie
all morning on the rock,
the sun burning through us,
the sand-filled wind whipping our skin.

For years in gray coastal cities we tensed our shoulders
and strode down illuminated avenues.
Doorways fell into shadow. Marquees
darkened the bars where couples leaned close
to talk below music, their breath
tentative in each other's ears.
All night, engines and sirens,

until neon dimmed
in the puddles and store windows
and the sky emerged flat, early light
that recalled us, blinking
gritty eyes, back to our own lives.

These are the names of our cities:
Los Alamos, Salt Lake City, Las Vegas,
Saint George. Late afternoon, southwest winds
brought storms and took them
in minutes. These names are from history:
Fat Boy, Diablo Canyon, Diablo,
Galileo, Trinity. The city
was safe. Mother
sent us out to take the air and sun.
The brief rains we opened our mouths to.

In the desert, a woman stepped out
to her porch. We didn't know this then.
We read it years later
as history. She walked out,
dried her hands on her apron,
leaned on the rail and looked west
over the desert, her hand shading
her eyes against the lowering sun.
Soon the atmosphere would refract
into red, violet. The colors of evening.

We were in school, the last hour,
learning of light, its weight
and substance, the particular waves
it travels by. She stood there,
lemonade in her hand. The ice cubes
shrank fast in the heat. She had never believed

it would be so white—brilliance
taking the whole sky. For a moment
she leaned toward it over the rail. She lost sight
of the moon, risen early, opaque
over the low hills. And the sun.
Nothing but that light
she turned from, palms pressed to her eyes.

If we were near home, mother
was calling us in, checking our faces,
behind our ears, the hands we held open.

We are almost settled.
Our childhood house
still perches on the hill, cool and familiar.
We listen to its lies.
The city pushes its old streets out
beyond the cultivated trees.
The desert glitters. From my window
we watch a cloud edge over the sun.
The cat on the sill twitches at birds
settling the closest limbs. The feeder
with its little sheltering eaves
you leaned high out over the pavement to hang for me,
your hands white-knuckled on the casement,
will have to hold them. The sparrows gather.
We drink lemonade as their voices
fade under rain's chipping at the glass.

We look sideways at each other's familiar profiles
or into our palms while we talk.
What we see—of course we love it
more than God does, who toys
with the shifting planet's center,
with the stars, their violent changes. Early
this morning, we found our neighborhood
almost as we'd left it. Brought in
the milk bottles, newspapers. Found we were left
our lives, altered so little
we didn't notice, bent down
and took them up again,
gently, in our hands.

The Suicides

for Janet

The leaves have never flown so beautifully.
They lie on the canyon roads like light.
There is no getting at the truth of this matter—
the season keeps vanishing into the cold air.

They lie on the canyon roads like light.
These friends insist on vanishing into the cold—
like the season, they keep vanishing into the cold air.
So we are left behind, alone, to cherish

all the friends who've vanished, leaving us cold.
This dizzying land, a city high in the air
is left behind for us alone to cherish,
all its ravaged, tree-lined neighborhoods.

This dizzying land, this city high in the air—
I will no longer look for perfection here.
Fall's ravaged all our tree-lined neighborhoods
and brought its flawed light to the houses.

I will no longer look for perfection here,
in this empty room we used to love.
Such a flawed light falls on the house
it hurts to breathe, to look across the valley.

So this has used our love, this empty room
we tend all night, keeping the lights turned high.
It hurts to breathe, to look across the valley,
so we turn away from the prospect;

keeping the lights turned high, we tend all night
an error of faith we must forgive.
We can only turn away from the prospect
where they've left everything so well done.

This error of faith we must forgive.
The leaves have never flown so beautifully,
have never left everything so well done.
There's no getting at the truth of this matter.

L.M., 1975; J.W., 1988; F.C., 1988

Before Parting

Neither of us can guess if they'll hurry
dusk along, those clouds that have loitered
all afternoon over the rooftops. From our window
the row of backyards appears, and one by one
sparrows lift from the trees and abandon

themselves to wind. No empty cupboard
sends me out in this weather to market,
but a restlessness, the storm,
and your notion of apples

completing the white bowl, candlelight
adrift on their skins. On the table, only that
lies between us, between our two knives
parting the meat; and after dinner we watch
every other moment the sky open

into fragile light. For those short illuminations
we hover near the window. We want each other
to believe that distance can't change us.
The sparrows also rustle, nervous,

returning to the eaves. When we pass them
over each other's bodies, our hands hesitate
as they never have, as if we considered
for the first time what might happen
to anything that leaves our fingers.

Kudzu

All along the highway in a deep southern light
it reaches up over the eaves of houses
bleached pearl-gray, over the fences
where women gossip, sweating in flowered dresses,
fanning themselves with straw fans
though it's April and the dogwood blossoms
still hover, pale and weightless, in the shade.
I tell myself this is charming—ease and decay,
an imported vine taking hold like habit
let loose: nails bitten to their bleeding quicks;
the hands of a lover who lost months ago
the loved body they still reach for all night;

a woman driving just to drive, as if
she could escape her own body
and the cells going wild inside it, leaving room
for less and less of her life. Each house is dying
in the rich, failing light. The women
step back inside, tie towels around their waists,
light their ovens, clean the fish and greens.
Their husbands come in laughing, and tonight
will touch them in ways that won't hurt. They don't
doubt what they know. I want to live
in a small, falling house, to walk down the highway
on Sundays, heat pounding through me,

and stand with a hymnal in vine-filtered light
and sing hymns I barely remember
about not knowing how to leave the world, about wanting
just to rise toward some unimaginable beginning.
Candles and lilies, approximate joy. A prayer
for the stuttering boy who hanged himself in his barn,
believing he'd ascend to God articulate, whole.
Sometimes we just cut out what is wrong.
The bruise from a pear. The potato's dark eyes.
The kudzu keeps growing back wilder.
The women thread their needles by lamplight
to mend what they can in their houses of leaves.

Demeter

I'm not waiting anymore. Not
waiting for anyone. This is

my creation, as much as
the barley or the silver wheat,

harvest, my face in the steamed window
fading. All this time

I've watched the earth die
into itself, this wind

that knows me. And under a high sky
birds knot and release

themselves to another season,
shadows pulling over the brief lawns.

So they live in a world grown
small—always, somewhere, the earth

pushes into green for them.
Their wings slacken, fold

under the weight of summer and all
that brilliance: scarlet throat

and flower, green, the mobile,
yellow eye. And I am small, like this valley

I color crystal, too fragile,
the people say, for their bodies'

burdens. They dream of traveling light
from the dying land, now there's nothing

to wait for, now they have wings
and go where the sun goes. They lie

in red and yellow dresses, lift
their faces to the heat. This is true

no matter what season. They fly
and land among strange trees

that remind them by different green
leaves of home. This afternoon

two deer browse my yard,
work the grass, my finished garden,

as they would grass rising thin
in the snow laid over the foothills.

The travelers grow restless and dull
and come back to the cold. No exile—

the land can't love one person
that much any more. Ice under the eaves

takes familiar shapes, changeable. The wind
comes like spring to another country—

houses for months snowed in
all the way to the rooftops, another kind

of exile. Hills darken behind me. Not
waiting. I look out,

poised on the edge. The deer, tender,
pull twigs from the shrubs, flowers gone

brittle, with care. All
as is. It will move me at least this long.

Touring the Yucatan

The sun turning overheard. The earth
in balance. We climb the pyramid,

counting, hands on the steps above.
We don't look down. The guide

goes ahead, for us
inventing history. We try to recall

the priest lifting a heart
to the sky, the blood still

moving it. Young girls, their eyes
black with botanical visions,

lying back in the sacred
waters. We each feel

that give, the decline
into pleasure. Dizzy, we close our eyes.

*

We stop in the village.
Children run up

selling Chiclets, panamas
we touch absently and pass by.

A girl leads us to the veranda,
brings iced drinks.

Plastic little birds perch on the glasses.
All around, birds chuckle,

flutter the branches, their heads
glowing bright from the shadows,

as if they agree
this world will do for us.

We raise our glasses,
pleased with them.

With how we transform
what pains us. The birdsong

comes as if from a distance,
cool, almost nostalgic.

*

Running hard, I leave the road.
The path, rough, force-

chipped from the hard ground,
leads into the jungle. Stones jut up.

Trees close around,
woven together above

by lianas thick as my arm.
In front of me, a dog snarls,

bares his teeth. I bend
for a stone, the gesture

alone turning him
back into the jungle,

to the man
I didn't see before. He wears

just the green of the shadow
the air casts under the trees.

He smokes. Holds his rifle
loose under his arm.

We watch each other: all
I know. He raises the rifle,

points it down the path
behind me, the way out.

*

Workers hack at the roots,
sinewy vines. Recover

temples, statues of gods
reclining or at war, the sacred rooms

where women pushed kings out
into the mysteries of water, sky,

their first breaths, their bodies.
The stones are replaced

one by one. Blue flowers
still come up between them. In the wind

the blossoms whirl, pulling
hard at their stems.

*

Equinox. Down
the pyramid's stone steps, light

snakes, a string of diamonds.
Now, we believe

this. The earth poises
straight on its axis

then evening.
The snake pulls back

stair by stair. Twilight
falls through the varied tiers

of leaves. We want to know how
they came to know light

so intimately. How many
gave up their vision, approaching

with eyes lifted up
that burning, godlike face.

Love Poem for the Nuclear Age
Utah, 1950—[   ]

"The sky is burning. I am shaking with cold."
Petrarch

Just the kind of disaster
we can't quite imagine
though we believe we can—
the city caught in a mirror
so empty it makes us tremble:
only the window behind
and the lights coming on
to waver across the valley.
I sit, combing my hair,
and look on from the edge
at a vast, silvered surface.

Think, for example, of poems of the fifties
written about eroding Italian fountains—
smoking hard, posing to fit in,
an American poet leaned propped under any frieze.
He wanted to fix the vacant-hearted *putti*,
playful, in his stark American mind.
He'd tried to leave that faulty land unlined—
just there, unformed, already vigorous, we
ticked codes in secret through our parents' cells,
already interrupted, muttering low.
Dawn's explosive moment. We can't quite
conceive; what was he doing? What in hell,
in the fallen world, was he out to show—
leaning, breathing the old, Italian light?

First, let's look at the *putti*.
Pink, their chubby folds
plump out the canvasses
glassed over and retouched
to ornament our museums—
the lavish moment of art

framed in humorous infants
looking on from the edge.
No other hiding place.
Where does collapse begin?
(Here, I'll help a little:
there's no barbarian tribe
coming for our young city.
The light of civilization
breaks on the horizon
nearer than we think.
It keeps gilding the windows.
How distant are the borders?)
This is what I mean

(darling, in the end I'll tell it all):
remember, as we traveled through the desert
toward the city, we saw its lights edging
the far horizon a hundred miles away.
An unsafe highway: our headlamps snagged the dark-
seeing eyes of small nocturnal mammals
huddled in the brush, beating like hearts.
Their eyes caught red as coals, fired, then faded.
More dangerous than the dark, our rising light
grows so vivid, so true, the animals run for it
and everything illuminated blinds them.
This morning, through the kitchen windows, mountains
burn with ice. We watch as long as we can
then turn away. It is too bright to see.

What mortal loveliness.
The city rings with ice
and I invent for us
this extravagant desert
undercut with faults
that bump and grind beneath.
Do *putti* peer from under
cacti frilled with blossoms?
Reader, art presumes,
but not to that extreme.
A long time coming, life.
This is what I mean:

Let's examine the *putti* carefully, shall we?
What is it that the poets want from them?—
perfect tourists, peering up the skirts
of oil-daubed, dead madonnas. Did I say vacant-
hearted? Vacant-headed, they hold the edge;
the essential thing: they never say a word,
and like most artful flirts, they don't put out.
The putti, *not the poets or the madonnas.*
Let's hold hands and stroll the galleries.
What stands of that constructed history?
How seriously we look on, poking our faces
in past the frames, toward the canvasses,
peripheral. And so we tour the world.
Stunning, it is beyond us. It has to do

with all there is of beauty.
If we admit the *putti*—
oh, forget it. Remember,
the city glimmers on
the lip of heaven, our own,
parched, ringed with mountains.
All will seem breathtaking
in retrospect, the earth
itself atremble, our hands
upheld against the impossible
sun, our skin ablaze.

The gallery window reflects the city street.
Behind us, a girl raises her arms—against
the stroke of love? The young man with his pants
pressed firm against her hip where it plumps out
into the bulge, tender, indiscreet,
that swells the hem of her shorts? Here, amongst
the window shoppers, remember the poet's angst,
the vision where he wanted to repeat
himself. Propped in the window, a Renaissance beauty
overflows the freshly printed surface,
her see-through nightie, into her own excess.
From each framed corner emerge the winged *putti*
to chasten, to uncover the virginal breast
her bridegroom eyes. He's still fully dressed.

Innocently, Dear Reader, as others have,
we've met, stepped from our separate frames to one,
touched each other's hands, then given in
to the promising distance of courtship. Why not? If we've
imagined the future poorly, we can't conceive
Italy, its ornamental seductions,
putti watching behind the weighty curtains.
Already fallen. A difference we believe.
The sun hefts its cold flame over the mountains,
taking its tender time. And this ache
that rises from our gestures as we watch
the window in our reflected faces: the skin
of ice goes to water, beads and breaks
the brittle membrane; the glass holds it, etched,

as we hold each other,
having committed what
the plot allowed, and having
called it love. Dear,
should we try to keep it?
Some things change the world
too much to believe.

Can you believe the burning sky? At last
it's inescapable. We step inside
the museum foyer and the fault slides.
Resonant artifacts tremble and chime as we pass,
and why not? Even the second best
will move us to focus, the stolen and falsified.
From frame to frame, the *putti* catch our eyes
and grow more lucid, their incidental gladness
webbing out like ice to glaze the glass.
Titian, for example, showing off,
brushed out this old imaginary painting
(the *putti* finally central, explode the canvas)
of Philastratus from mere words into life.
(Legs entwined with legs. The infants' panting

kisses. Venus watches.)
The gaze we bring into

this century: a room,
a kitchen window we rise
to look through in the morning—
no apocalypse,
just regular houses burning
the same porch lights all day.
How long it takes to arrive,
your hand pressing my back.
The *putti* watch us, gleeful,
vacant, beyond us all.
Their foreheads press the membrane.
Mobile, dying, full,
the heart beneath my breast
opens and closes hard.
What is the essential thing?
The future's brilliant surface
glitters still (look hard
now at my face): its violence
drives us on.

*Katharine Coles left the state of her birth, Utah, to attend the University of Washington and the University of Houston, earning a B.A. at the first institution and an M.A. at the second. After serving as Writer-in-Residence at St. Albans School (the National Cathedral School for boys) in Washington, D.C., she returned to Utah to earn a Ph.D. in Creative Writing at the University of Utah in Salt Lake City. Currently, Katharine Coles is an Assistant Professor of English at Westminster College. Her work has appeared in numerous magazines and journals, including poems in **The New Republic**, **The Georgia Review**, **Shenandoah**, **College English**, and **Prairie Schooner**, and fiction in **North American Review**, **Alaska Quarterly Review**, and **Rariton**. She has received grants and awards from the National Endowment for the Arts, PEN, the Utah Arts Council, the D.C. Commission on the Arts and Humanities, the Academy of American Poets, and other organizations. Works in progress include freelance projects, a novel, and poems written in the context of a collaboration with painter Maureen O'Hara Ure.*

Ahsahta Press

MODERN & CONTEMPORARY POETRY
OF THE AMERICAN WEST

Sandra Alcosser, *A Fish To Feed All Hunger*
David Axelrod, *Jerusalem of Grass*
*David Baker, *Laws of the Land*
*Conger Beasley, Jr., *Over DeSoto's Bones*
 Linda Bierds, *Flights of the Harvest Mare*
 Richard Blessing, *Winter Constellations*
*Peggy Pond Church, *New & Selected Poems*
 Katharine Coles, *The One Right Touch*
 Wyn Cooper, *The Country of Here Below*
*Judson Crews, *The Clock of Moss*
 H. L. Davis, *Selected Poems*
*Susan Strayer Deal, *The Dark Is a Door*
                              No Moving Parts
*Gretel Ehrlich, *To Touch the Water*
 Julie Fay, *Portraits of Women*
*Thomas Hornsby Ferril, *Anvil of Roses*
                              Westering
*Hildegarde Flanner, *The Hearkening Eye*
 Charley John Greasybear, *Songs*
 Corrinne Hales, *Underground*
 Hazel Hall, *Selected Poems*
 Nan Hannon, *Sky River*
 Gwendolen Haste, *Selected Poems*
 Kevin Hearle, *Each Thing We Know Is Changed Because We Know It*
                              And Other Poems
 Sonya Hess, *Kingdom of Lost Waters*
 Cynthia Hogue, *The Woman in Red*
*Robert Krieger, *Headlands, Rising*
 Elio Emiliano Ligi, *Disturbances*
 Haniel Long, *My Seasons*
*Norman Macleod, *Selected Poems*
 Ken McCullough, *Sycamore•Oriole*
 Barbara Meyn, *The Abalone Heart*
 Dixie Partridge, *Deer in the Haystacks*

Gerrye Payne, *The Year-God*
George Perreault, *Curved Like An Eye*
Howard W. Robertson, *to the fierce guard in the Assyrian Saloon*
*Leo Romero, *Agua Negra*
                 Going Home Away Indian
Philip St. Clair, *At the Tent of Heaven*
                 Little-Dog-Of-Iron
Donald Schenker, *Up Here*
Gary Short, *Theory of Twilight*
*Richard Speakes, *Hannah's Travel*
Genevieve Taggard, *To the Natural World*
*Marnie Walsh, *A Taste of the Knife*
Bill Witherup, *Men at Work*
*Carolyne Wright, *Stealing the Children*

Women Poets of the West: An Anthology, 1850-1950

*Selections from these volumes, read by their authors, are available on *The Ahsahta Cassette Sampler.*